and

THE GLYN VALLEY TRAMWAY

A Portrait in Old Picture Postcards

by
Verna Palmer

S. B. Publications
1988

First published in 1988 by S. B. Publications.

Reprinted January 1989

5 Queen Margaret's Road, Loggerheads, Nr. Market Drayton, Shropshire, TF9 4EP.

© Copyright S. B. Publications 1988.

All rights reserved.

ISBN 1 870708 03 2

Printed and bound in Great Britain by Rubell Print Ltd., Bunbury, Tarporley, Cheshire, CW6 9PQ.

CONTENTS

Page

Introduction

Acknowledgements and Bibliography

CHIRK

Chirk Village	1 – 3
Station Road, Chirk	4 – 6
War Memorial and Playing Fields	7
Chirk Castle	8
Chirk Castle Gates	9
Chirk AAA Football Club	10
Chirk Hospital	11
Parish Hall and Girls' School, Chirk	12
St. Mary's Church	13 – 14
Brynkinalt	15
Chirk Mill	16
Chirk Bridge	17
The Canal, Aqueduct and Viaduct	18 – 20
Chirk Station	21

CONTENTS CONTINUED
THE GLYN VALLEY TRAMWAY

	Page
Map of the Glyn Valley Tramway	22
An outline history of the Glyn Valley Tramway	23
'Our Local Train'	24
Pontfaen Farm and Yew Tree Cottages	25
Pontfaen Station	26
The Fisheries, Chirk	27
Castle Mill	28
Pontfadog	29 – 33
Dolywern	34 – 35
The Star Inn and Pear Tree Cottage	36
Glyn Ceiriog	37 – 39
The Glyn Valley Trains	40 – 43
Glyn Ceiriog, general view	44
The Station, Glyn Ceiriog	45 – 48
The Cross, Glyn Ceiriog	49 – 50
High Street, Glyn Ceiriog	51
The Glyn Valley Hotel	52 – 53
Glyn 'Spurs'	54
Gorsedd Eisteddfod Talaith Powys, Glyn Ceiriog	55
The Post Office, Glyn Ceiriog	56
Brookside Glyn	57
Glyn Ceiriog	58
The Bridge, Glyn Ceiriog	59
Ceiriog River	60
The Station, Glyn Ceiriog	61
The Late Glyn Valley Train	62
Llanarmon D. C.	63 – 66

INTRODUCTION

This book is an attempt to give, through postcards, a glimpse of the people who lived and worked in the valley of the River Ceiriog along with the buildings, industries and transport that existed there in the first few decades of this century.

Our postcard tour begins in Chirk, at the eastern end of the valley close to where the River Ceiriog joins the River Dee, and continues for almost fifteen miles to Llanarmon Dyffryn Ceiriog, just south of the Ceiriog Falls which mark the river's source. Postcards of the villages and hamlets along the route, Chirk, Pontfaen, Castle Mill, Pontfadog, Dolywern, Glyn Ceiriog and Llanarmon are featured and they illustrate the history and development of one of the prettiest industrial valleys in Wales.

Many thousands of postcards of the Ceiriog Valley were published and posted during the first decades of this century and they provide a valuable record of the social history of an area, which has seen a vast amount of change. The mills, the mines and a tramway may have gone but they lasted long enough to be recorded on postcards for future generations to study and enjoy, and which are collected as highly prized records of a bygone era today.

I hope you will enjoy this peep into the past and short postcard tour, and be encouraged to see for yourselves this delightful Welsh valley that was once blessed with a very special little tramway.

Verna Palmer
January, 1988

ACKNOWLEDGEMENTS

The author wishes to thank those residents of the Ceiriog Valley and Chirk, who have helped identify people and places featured on these postcards.

The Oakwood Press, Headington, Oxford, for their very kind permission to reproduce the map on page 22, previously published in 'The Glyn Valley Tramway' by David Llewellyn Davies.

Editorial and marketing: Steve Benz.

BIBLIOGRAPHY

Glyn Valley Tramway by David Llewellyn Davies : Oakwood Press
The Ceiriog : Denbighshire, N. Wales by David Llewellyn Davies : published by the author.
Various Guides to Chirk Castle, Glyn Ceiriog and North Wales.

Also published by S. B. Publications:

Chesterfield: A portrait in old picture postcards
Bootle: A portrait in old picture postcards
Chester: A portrait in old picture postcards

CHIRK VILLAGE, c. 1908
The village of Chirk is known in Welsh as Y Waun (moorland), but the name Chirk is possibly a derivation of the word Ceiriog. Once owned by the Myddelton family, the village was sold by auction in 1911, two years after this postcard was posted.
Since this view of the village, from the south, was taken the houses on the left hand side have been converted into shops and the first house on the right is now an estate agents.

CHIRK VILLAGE, c. 1905

The road along which motorists pass through Chirk on their way to the North Wales coastal resorts is the turnpike road built by Telford in 1826, which improved the mail service between Holyhead and London. The mail coach passed along Church Street at 9 pm each evening and although the 16th century Hand Hotel, on the left, was not an official stopping place for the mail coach, it was used by other travellers. Taken from the north, this view shows the gates at the side of the inn through which horses and coaches entered.

CHIRK VILLAGE, c. 1909
An interesting photograph of Church Street showing the old cottages beyond the Hand Hotel on the left hand side, most of which have since been converted into shops. Chirk Post Office occupies the corner site on the right, which was later taken over by Chirk and District Co-operative Society and is, today a large craft and gift shop.

STATION ROAD, CHIRK, c. 1908
A view of Station Road (Avenue) from the Hand Hotel looking towards the Station and Castle. The individual units of the building on the left have since been converted into one large shop premises and the neat row of railings on the right hand side have been removed.

STATION ROAD AND HAND HOTEL, CHIRK, c. 1930
The War Memorial has been erected and the row of shops on the right hand side of Station Road includes a Newsagents, E. Jones, and a Chemists where today there is an opticians. The Newsagents was also the Post Office for a time, following its transfer from the corner site.

STATION ROAD, CHIRK, c. 1909
This postcard shows a neat hedge on the left hand side and on the right,
the picturesque cottages which, before being demolished,
stood on the site of the present day 'Ye Old Smithy Cafe' car park.

WAR MEMORIAL AND PLAYING FIELDS, CHIRK, c. 1920's
A view of the Playing Fields behind the war memorial.
Since this photograph was taken a row of trees has been planted, thus obscuring the view and a bus shelter has been erected on the left hand side of the road.

CHIRK CASTLE, c. 1920

Chirk Castle was built in 1310 by Roger Mortimer to defend his newly created Lordship of Chirk. This Marcher Lordship, which included the Ceiriog Valley and Llangollen, lasted until 1536 when it was absorbed into the county of Denbigh. The home of the Myddelton family since 1595, it is the only border castle to have been continuously occupied since being built and the outside has remained virtually unaltered. The castle now belongs to the National Trust.

CHIRK CASTLE GATES, c. 1920
These gates, which have been at the main entrance to Chirk Castle since 1888, were made by the Davies brothers of Bersham. They are a fine example of decorative wrought ironwork for which the Wrexham area was well known and were first erected nearer to the castle in 1719.

CHIRK AAA FOOTBALL CLUB, 1919-1920
A photograph of the successful Chirk AAA football team of the 1919-1920 season with their trophies. These included the St. Martins Cup (1919) and the Oswestry and District League Cup (1918-1919).

CHIRK HOSPITAL, c. 1921
Chirk Hospital opened in August, 1921 with room for up to 18 patients,
and closed on 30th October, 1987.
Most of the buildings will be demolished to make way for a new hospital
which is expected to open in March, 1990.

PARISH HALL AND GIRLS' SCHOOL, CHIRK, c. 1908
This postcard was published not long after these buildings were built in 1902.
Sent by Beta who attended the school, the message mentions that she was going to sing in the Hall, on the left, later in the month.
The Hall is used for meetings and local functions, while the school has a new lease of life as a warehouse.

ST. MARY'S CHURCH, CHIRK, c. 1905
A view taken from Castle Road, showing St. Mary's Church, with its 15th century tower and roof. Since this postcard was published the cottages on the left have been converted into shops and the arch over the entrance to the Churchyard has been replaced by a Lych gate.

DEDICATION OF THE LYCH GATE, 1923
The Lych Gate was erected by the friends of Lt. Colonel John Lloyd and his wife, who had lived at 'The Mount', Chirk, in memory of his service as local doctor for forty years.
This photograph shows the crowds present when the Lych Gate was dedicated in 1923.

BRYNKINALT, c. 1920's
Brynkinalt, home of the Trevor family, was built in 1619 and portions are believed to have been designed by Inigo Jones.
The Duke of Wellington spent some of his holidays here as a child since it was the home of his grandmother, Viscountess Dungannon.

CHIRK MILL, c. 1909
Chirk Mill, one of a dozen or so watermills in use at one time along the banks
of the River Ceiriog, was used for grinding corn as early as 1495.
Last used as a corn mill in 1941, the buildings are now occupied by small workshops.
The cottages on the right have been demolished.

CHIRK BRIDGE, c. 1905
This bridge carries the main A5 road over the River Ceiriog to the south of Chirk. The two buildings on the left have been demolished but the Bridge Inn, in Shropshire, on the right, has changed little since this postcard was published, when people in Wales had to cross over the border to buy a drink here on a Sunday.

THE CANAL, CHIRK, c. 1930
Chirk Aqueduct was built in 1801 by Thomas Telford to carry the Shropshire Union Canal 65 feet above the Ceiriog Valley in an iron trough set in the stone. This postcard shows the $\frac{1}{4}$ mile long tunnel at the northern end, built to preserve the view from and access roads to the Castle, and which, unlike many others, was built with a towpath so that the boatmen did not have the hard work of 'legging' their barges through.

AQUEDUCT AND VIADUCT, CHIRK, c. 1916
The Shrewsbury to Chester railway line was opened to passenger traffic on
12th October, 1848 after a viaduct had been built, alongside, but 35 ft higher than,
the aqueduct over the Ceiriog valley.
This 1916 postcard shows a Shrewsbury bound GWR engine.

THE CANAL, CHIRK, c. 1933
An interesting postcard showing the canal and wharf at Chirk Bank.
The brick building and the lifting equipment, used for transferring loads have long since been removed, the canal last being used commercially in the mid 1940's.
At one time the canal connected with the Glyn Valley Tramway at Gledrid and, further north, to a tramway which brought coal from Black Park Colliery.

CHIRK STATION N.W., c. 1918

Chirk Station, on the main G.W.R. Shrewsbury–Chester line, was known at one time as Hand Lane Station, and lies in a cutting alongside the road running from Chirk Castle to the Hand Hotel. The Glyn Valley Tramway also had a station here, the narrow gauge line running alongside the standard gauge G.W.R. track. The tall G.W.R. station building on the left hand side has recently been demolished and replaced by a small stone shelter.

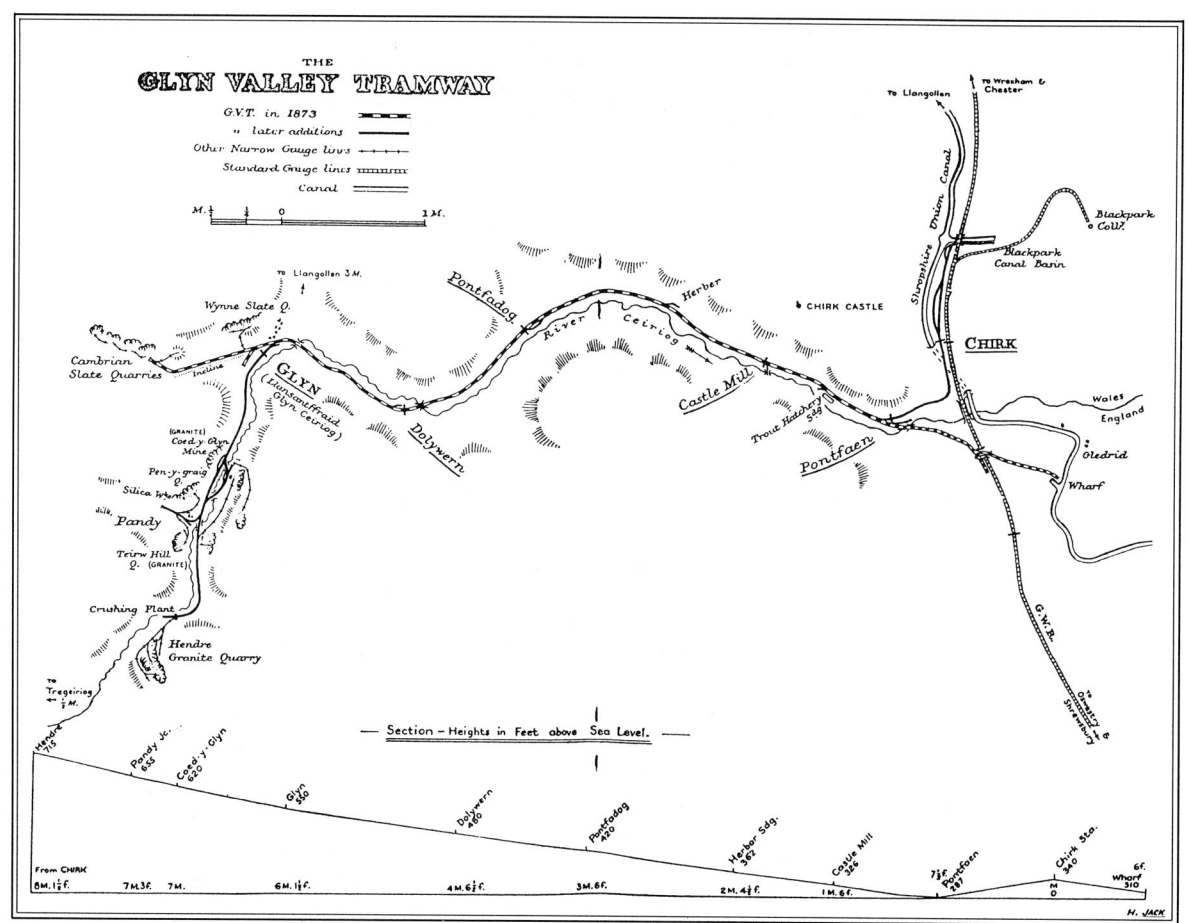

AN OUTLINE HISTORY OF
THE GLYN VALLEY TRAMWAY

From Chirk our postcard tour follows the river westwards along the 'exquisite little valley of the Ceiriog' to quote David Lloyd George. The road along which we travel was completed in 1863, being built wide enough to run a tramway alongside at a later date. Until 1888, tolls were collected at Chirk, Herber and Glyn Ceiriog.

In 1870, The Glyn Valley Tramway Act gave permission for a horse drawn tramway to run alongside the new road, linking Glyn Ceiriog with the canal at Gledrid. Operated by the Shropshire Union Railway and Canal Co, it had a unique 2' 4¼" gauge which was exactly half the standard gauge, and which, when the line was converted to steam had to be relaid ¼" wider. Although built to bring slate, granite and other minerals down the valley, the tramway returned with essentials like coal and flour.

When the Tramway was converted to steam in 1888 a new station was built at Glyn Ceiriog, the line was extended westwards to Hendre granite quarry and re-routed eastwards to the G.W.R. station at Chirk. It was now roughly 8 miles long.

The Tramway relied heavily on the revenue from carrying granite so when the demand for granite declined after the First World War and road transport proved more flexible, both for freight and passengers, the Glyn Valley Tramway was unable to keep going. After seeing the passenger service axed in 1933, the line was closed to all traffic on 6th July, 1935. It had been in existence for just 62 years.

The postcards feature several items of the Tramway that can be seen in the valley today. The ticket offices at Dolywern, Pontfadog and Glyn Ceiriog are still standing, together with the engine shed at Glyn Ceiriog, whilst the bridge built to carry the steam trains over the river at Dolywern is visible through the trees. Although all the engines were sold for scrap, two of the coaches have been restored and are running on the Talyllyn Railway. In the upper valley, near Hendre, a walk has been established along the route the line used to take. At both the Wynne Slate Quarry and the Memorial Institute many relics of the slate industry and the tramway are on display.

'OUR LOCAL TRAIN', c. 1908
Today the only means of transport along the Ceiriog Valley is by road, but for 62 years, from 1873 until 1935 there was also, at least as far as Glyn Ceiriog, a little tramway. The name of the train on this postcard is hardly appropriate, however, for a train which took a little under one hour to cover the six mile journey, besides which, the Tramways Act stipulated — no passengers on the roof!

PONTFAEN FARM AND YEW TREE COTTAGES, CHIRK, c. 1900's
In its early days the tramway was horse drawn and to reach the canal near Gledrid from Glyn Ceiriog, it had to cross the River Ceiriog over a wooden bridge at Pontfaen where the number of wagons had to be reduced to enable the horse to pull them up the steep bank near the farm on the right. When the line was converted to steam, it was allowed to cross the Chirk Castle estate to gain access to the G.W.R. Station at Chirk and this section was abandoned.

PONTFAEN STATION, GLYN VALLEY TRAMWAY, c. 1905
After making its way down the steep bank from the station at Chirk, the train crossed over the road and made its first stop at Pontfaen, which, as can be seen from this card, had neither platform nor waiting room. Between 1900 and 1933, Third Class passengers paid 8d. for the 6 mile journey to Glyn Ceiriog, with stops being made at Castle Mill, Pontfadog and Dolywern.

THE FISHERIES, CHIRK, c. 1907
From Pontfaen the track ran alongside the Fish Hatchery, built in 1901 with twelve fish ponds, where there was a small siding.
Live fish were sometimes transported in milk churns.
The Hatchery, on the left, still produces trout for stocking the Dee and Ceiriog rivers as well as for private pools and streams.

CASTLE MILL, c. 1930
Castle Mill, the next stop along the valley, was named after the castle and its corn mill
which was in use from 1398 until the late 18th century.
Although most of the mills along the valley were corn mills others were used for
fulling, iron forging, flannel and gunpowder making.
Local residents can just be seen in the porches of the cottages
which show little change today.

PONTFADOG, GLYN VALLEY.   "The Unique Series".

PONTFADOG, c. 1905
The hamlet of Pontfadog (Madoc's Bridge) showing the church, built in 1892, the partly hidden post office and behind it the Swan Inn.
Many houses have been built alongside the Inn since this photograph was taken and the small buildings on the right hand side have been demolished.

PONTFADOG, c. 1909
The small red brick building, on the left of this postcard, was Pontfadog Station which combined as a waiting room and ticket office for the tramway.
Built on the opposite side of the road to the line, it had no platform, and has since been converted into 'The Little Shop' and painted white.

PONTFADOG, c. 1909
Looking towards Pontfadog from Chirk and showing the loop where trains could pass each other on the single line track.
Today, bushes partly obscure this view of the river and a garage and many houses have been built along the right hand side of the road.
The post office in the distance can be seen without its porch and extension.

THE BIG OAK, PONTFADOG,
c. 1909
The Big Oak at Pontfadog, credited on this card with being the largest oak tree in the United Kingdom with a girth of 17 yards, is still a remarkable sight today, even though sections have broken off over the years. Believed to be over 1000 years old, the trunk is hollow.

TRAMWAYS, PONTFADOG VILLAGE, c. 1920
Another interesting photograph of Pontfadog village.
A mixed train, on its way to Chirk, is laden with 15 granite waggons which,
by the 1890's, had replaced slate as the most important mineral produced in the valley.

DOLYWERN, c. 1908
Showing the road through the centre of the village along which the horse trams used to pass. These bends were too sharp for the steam locomotives to negotiate so an alternative route had to be found.
The Leonard Cheshire Home, originally the Queen Hotel, is on the right hand side of the road and several new wings have been added recently.

DOLYWERN, c. 1910
This card shows how the track was straightened to go around the village.
A new steel bridge carried the line over the river and is still visible
through the trees today. Also shown in the centre is the small red brick waiting room,
which is still standing, but sadly neglected.

THE STAR INN AND PEAR TREE COTTAGE, c. 1930's
The Star Inn seen on the left and now a private residence, provided refreshment and accommodation for visitors to the valley.
The line can be seen passing just in front of the Inn on the road itself.

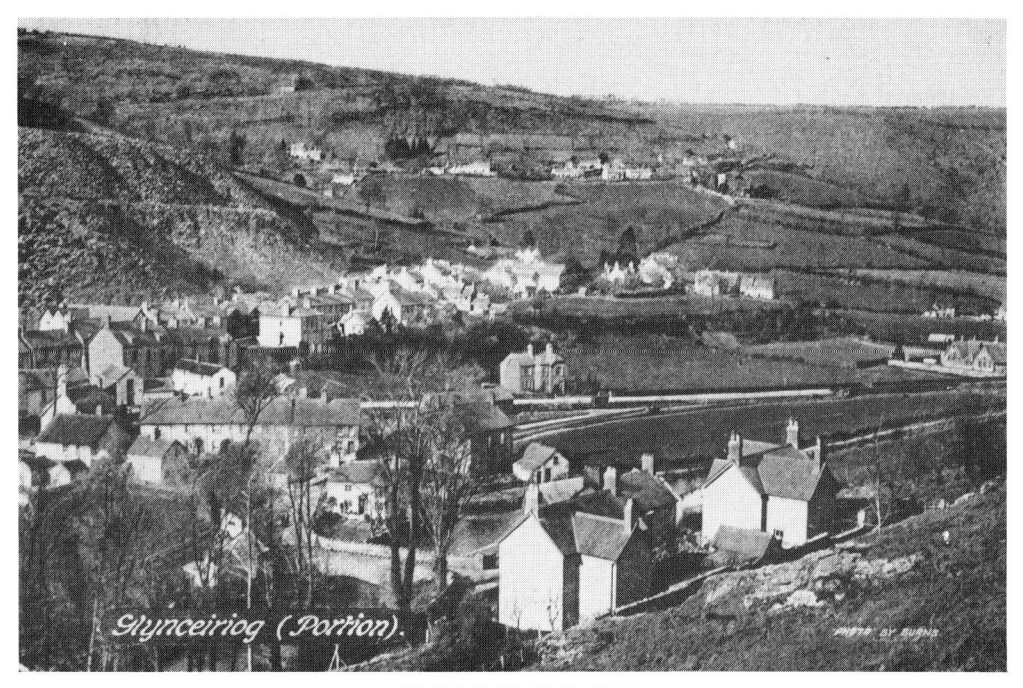

GLYN CEIRIOG, 1910
Llansantffraid Glyn Ceiriog, the western terminus of the Glyn Valley Tramway, was producing slate as early as the 16th century and the original village was established on the hillside close to the church. The modern village, shown in the mid-distance with the Wynne slate quarry towering above it, owes it existence to the turnpike road and resultant increase in slate production and to the tramway which brought prosperity to the area for a short time.

GLYN SLATE QUARRY, GLYN CEIRIOG, c. 1905
The two main slate quarries were the Wynne Quarry which overlooked Glyn Ceiriog itself and was in operation until 1927 and the Cambrian Slate Quarry which continued to produce slate until 1947. Although they both began as quarries, by 1900 they had been converted into mines with around 300 men extracting the slate by candlelight.

THE CROSS, GLYN CEIRIOG, c. 1930
Although slate was plentiful the mines were rather isolated, so when the Shropshire Union Canal reached Gledrid in 1797, plans were put forward to build a tramway to connect the quarries with the canal and markets further afield. However, it was 80 years before the first horse drawn trams, went into service in 1873, running alongside the new turnpike road and pulling into a wooden terminus just outside the New Inn (Glyn Valley Hotel), where these trucks are standing.

39

THE GLYN VALLEY TRAIN, c. 1909
In 1888, the line was converted to steam and the first locomotives to be purchased were the 'Sir Theodore', shown here, which was named after Sir Theodore Martin, Chairman of the Company from 1886-1909 and the 'Dennis', purchased in 1889, which took its name from Henry Dennis, Engineer and a Director of the Company. Both cost £1,200.

THE GLYN VALLEY TRAIN, c. 1909
The first trains carried freight only but when passengers were allowed in the 1890's, open coaches were purchased at a cost of £60 each.
It was not until later that the ends were boarded up so that in 1909, these passengers would have been in for quite a draughty journey!

THE 'GLYN', c. 1906

In 1892, a third locomotive, 'Glyn' was purchased, seen here at Glyn Ceiriog around 1906. It can be distinguished from the earlier engines by the maker's name plate which is on the rear of the cab instead of the front.

THE 'GLYN', c. 1906
Another postcard of the locomotive 'Glyn' with wagons laden with minerals
in the background.
Like the other locomotives, the 'Glyn' was scrapped when the line closed.

GLYN CEIRIOG, GENERAL VIEW, c. 1906
In the mid-distance, behind the four coaches, can be seen the booking office with the engine shed alongside. The engine shed is still in a fair condition while the waiting room has been converted into a house.
The river is in the foreground and the Wynne slate quarry, with its many small buildings and incline, dominates the area behind the village.

THE STATION, GLYN CEIRIOG, c. 1909
A closer look at the station and showing a train waiting by the Platform. Although the mineral line extended beyond Glyn Ceiriog, through the gate in the foreground, passengers had to alight here.
Still in position, a barrier of trees has now been built in front of this gate.

THE STATION, GLYN CEIRIOG, c. 1906
The 'Sir Theodore' waiting at Glyn Ceiriog to leave for Chirk.
The building shown behind the train is on the opposite side of the track
to the waiting room and platform.

THE STATION, GLYN CEIRIOG, c. 1905
This view, looking towards Glyn Ceiriog, shows the track to the left running into the station and to the right, the line to the Cambrian and Wynne slate quarries which was also the line to the horse tramway station. The engine shed is on the left and houses have since been built along both sides of the road.

47

THE STATION, GLYN CEIRIOG, c. 1910
A view of the station looking in the direction of Chirk, for which a train is just about to leave. The once open coaches on the right have had their sides boarded up to make them less draughty and the old school, which has since been demolished, can be seen on the left.

THE CROSS, GLYN CEIRIOG, c. 1909
This postcard shows two sets of lines, the one to the left going to the slate quarries, the one to the right to the siding on the site of the old horse tram terminus. The buildings in the centre have since been rebuilt and are now occupied by the Midland Bank.

THE CROSS, GLYN CEIRIOG, c. 1908
A view of the Cross before the building of either the Memorial Institute in 1911 or the War Memorial in 1921.
The shop on the right hand side, which was demolished in the early 1930's, belongs to Edwards and Davies, General Drapers and to its left can be seen the slate trucks on their way down from the quarries to the station.

HIGH STREET, GLYN CEIRIOG, c. 1911
A view of High Street with the line to the slate quarries shown in the foreground. On the left, the Cross Stores has boots and shoes, glass and china for sale while the shop behind the signpost is occupied by T. Griffiths, Newsagents.
This shop is now occupied by an antique dealer.
The Memorial Institute, built as a tribute to several local poets, can also be seen.

THE GLYN VALLEY HOTEL, c. 1908
The Glyn Valley Hotel was built in 1835 and was originally called the New Inn;
its name being changed to the present one around 1900.
Looking towards Llanarmon, this photograph shows the early horse tramway terminus
on the left hand side being used as a siding and goods yard while on the right,
a horse drawn delivery cart can be seen.

THE GLYN VALLEY HOTEL, c. 1905
Although most trains were mixed, on certain days passenger only trains would run and this elegant group could well have arrived this way. One popular excursion was to travel from Llangollen to Chirk along the canal and thence by the tramway to Glyn Ceiriog with the more energetic walking back over the hills if they so wished.

GLYN 'SPURS', (1920-21)
This postcard shows the Glyn 'Spurs' football team of the 1920-1921 season.
Most of the players worked at one of the quarries and are believed to be,
Back row: T. Roberts (Lawson), T. O. Hughes, D. Jones, (not known), A. Evans, G. Evans.
Front row: D. Evans, H. Edwards, T. Hughes, B. Roberts, T. Brown.
Jack Davies and Jack Jones are standing either side of the players.

GORSEDD EISTEDDFOD TALAITH POWYS, GLYN CEIRIOG, 22nd Sept., 1928
Published by T. E. Hughes of the Post Office, this postcard shows the Powys Eisteddfod when it was the turn of Glyn Ceiriog to host the event in 1928.
The event took place on the field in front of the Glyn Valley Hotel and in the background to the left, is the Hotel Garage and to the right, the old horse tramway shed. Many of these visitors could have arrived by tramway, although by this time more and more people were travelling by bus.

THE POST OFFICE, GLYN CEIRIOG, c. 1915
Published by the postmaster T. E. Hughes, this card shows the Post Office with a quartet of schoolboys posing in front and the horse tramway shed to the right. The Post Office has changed little since this photograph was taken, although the wall has disappeared and the road has been widened.

BROOKSIDE GLYN, c. 1910
An interesting postcard showing a group of villagers (and one dog) lined up for the photographer outside the oldest houses in the Ceiriog Valley.
These cottages were demolished in the 1920's and the site has since been redeveloped.

GLYN CEIRIOG, c. 1906
When the Glyn Valley Tramway was converted to steam the line was extended to bring granite, chinastone, silica and other minerals from the quarries at Hendre, Pandy and Treirw. This postcard shows the gate, in the centre mid-distance, through which trains passed in and out of the station. The Cambrian quarry, now covered by trees on land owned by the Forestry Commission, lies behind the trees to the left of the picture.

THE BRIDGE, GLYN CEIRIOG,
c. 1908
Looking through the trees and over the bridge reveals wagons laden with stone from the upper valley quarries about to enter Glyn Ceiriog station, just out of the picture on the right. Hendre stone was mainly used in road building and over 3 million tons were extracted altogether.
The Glyn Valley Hotel can be seen in the background.

CEIRIOG RIVER, GLYN CEIRIOG N.W., c. 1912
The track left the road and ran alongside the river for the 2 miles or so to Hendre. By 1900, granite was by far the most important mineral carried and was a vital source of revenue for the G.V.T.. When the tonnage of granite carried declined, the Glyn Valley Tramway could no longer keep going and the Company was wound up in 1935. Hendre quarry itself closed in 1950.

THE STATION, GLYN CEIRIOG, 1934
A final look at a rather desolate station, ticket office and waiting room,
just one year after the line closed to passenger traffic.
To the left of the waiting room, a solitary worker can be seen.
Increased competition from buses and private cars meant that between 1911 and 1932
the number of passengers travelling on the tramway fell from 39,000 a year to just over
13,000 and the service was no longer economically viable.

THE LATE GLYN VALLEY TRAIN, c. 1936
The caption to the postcard indicates that there was a demand for cards showing the tramway even after the line had closed. Published by T. E. Hughes of the Post Office, this is a reprint of an earlier photograph.
After the line closed in 1935, the track was removed and taken to Gresford colliery to be used in new workings opened up to replace those sealed after the recent disastrous fire.

THE POST OFFICE, LLANARMON D. C., c. 1920

The Ceiriog Falls form the source of the River Ceiriog just four miles north of the village of Llanarmon Dyffryn Ceiriog.

The postcard shows the Post Office in the centre while in the building to the right, with the wheel in front, the local blacksmith can be seen at work.

THE WEST ARMS INN, LLANARMON D. C., c. 1910
This postcard shows an interesting group of men, possibly a shooting party,
lined up for the photographer outside the West Arms Inn, around 1910.
The West Arms was built in the 18th century and still retains much of its old character.

PENYBRYN, LLANARMON D. C., c. 1910
Penybryn, Llanarmon was the home of the poet Ceiriog, of whom the valley is very proud. John Ceiriog Hughes worked for the Oswestry Advertizer as a printer before moving to Manchester, eventually returning to Wales to work as a railway clerk in Powys. He won the Chair at the National Eisteddfod at Llangollen in 1848 for his poem Myfanwy Fychan. He died in 1887, aged 55, and is buried at Llanwnog, near Caersws. Since this postcard was published a plaque has been mounted at the side of the doorway.

THE CEIRIOG CENTENARY HALL, LLANARMON D. C., c. 1932
The Ceiriog Centenary Hall was built to celebrate the centenary of the birth of
John Ceiriog Hughes (Ceiriog) in 1932.
The Church, dedicated to St. Garmon, was rebuilt in 1846.